This will give you
a chance to see a little
more of Australia.
        Love, Ann and Bob

Don Dunstan's Australia

Don

Dunstan's Australia

Photographs by Julia Featherstone

RIGBY

My thanks go to Anne Macmahon for typing the manuscript.

Julia Featherstone thanks Avis Rent A Car System Pty Ltd and Trans Australia Airlines for their help and co-operation, which made her travels so pleasurable; and George's Camera Store Pty Ltd and Maxwell Photo-Optics for their expert advice and assistance with Nikon camera equipment.

The extract from the poem My Country is reproduced by permission of the Estate of Dorothea Mackellar, c/- Curtis Brown (Aust) Pty Ltd, Sydney

RIGBY LIMITED • ADELAIDE • SYDNEY
MELBOURNE • BRISBANE • PERTH

Dunstan, Donald Allan
  Don Dunstan's Australia

  ISBN 0 7270 0901

  1. Australia—history. I. Featherstone,
  Julia, photographer. II. Title.

994

First published 1978
Text copyright © 1978 D. A. Dunstan
Photographs copyright © 1978 Julia Featherstone
All rights reserved

Wholly produced in Adelaide, South Australia.
Typeset by Modgraphic Pty Ltd. Colour separations by Stock Journal
Publishers Pty Ltd. Printed by Commercial Printing House Pty Ltd.
Bound by Advance Bookbinders Pty Ltd.

Also by Don Dunstan
Don Dunstan's Cookbook

Title page illustration: The Adelaide Festival Centre

Contents

1

Home Thoughts, from Abroad

This is in many ways a love story. And for many it will be too objective, critical, or analytical to be so. Isn't love, however, most truly love when it is *not* blind?

My parents were Australians. But I was born and brought up in Fiji, so that the landscapes in which I felt at home were firstly the tropical—the lush verdure of rain trees, vaus, bamboos, bananas, coconuts and palms; the steaming jungle of tropical rain forest, interlaced with liana; the warm humid air, the extravagance of growth and brilliance of colour I grew up to feel my own. In great love there is no staleness. When you take your love in your arms there is always the shock of surprised recognition of how beautiful and right that is. And for me that same shock of surprise, delight and at-homeness occurs when I see the environment of my childhood again.

I was at school and university in Australia during the years 1940–5, and at the end of 1945 I contrived to go back to Fiji to see my parents. On the train, in a second-class carriage of the Overland to Sydney, there was a photograph of tropical forest on the wall, the first I had seen for years. It struck me with immediate force: a longing for the sights, sounds, smells, feel of the place where I had been born. It was an intense yearning and nostalgia, which come back to me whenever I

In the Australian tropics, Cairns

remember the incident these thirty-odd years later. In Australia, I recapture my delight in tropical landscapes by visiting northern Queensland.

The *other* landscape I knew was from pictures and I suppose a kind of race-consciousness. It was the English—not the Australian—countryside. How did it happen that I felt so at home there? Was it merely because the books I read as a child assumed 'home' to be England and often were illustrated with English scenes, and that the picture books and jigsaw puzzles over which I pored and laboured were of Constable-like scenes of the English countryside? I find it hard to define how this sense of identity with England came to be mine. But I felt it unmistakeably, as did very many Australians of English descent.

A sunburnt country. In the Kimberley, WA

Australia then, to me, was a shock. When I came on trips to this country as a small boy, first when I was two, then five, and then at seven to stay for three years, I found the landscape arid, stony, angular, and uncomfortable. The towns and cities were much larger and more crowded than anything I had known, and that added of course to the sense of strangeness and of not belonging. Perhaps, too, that sense was compounded by the fact that my grandmother and aunts lived at Murray Bridge, a country town in South Australia. In those days the town was not picturesque. And they were descendants of original settlers at Monarto, an arid, shallow valley with little vegetation except low mallee scrub, where I was taken for church reunions. I was scared by constantly new scenes and strange machines. I electrified the store of Charles Birks in Adelaide (now David Jones) at age two by shrieking in Fijian '*Raica na waqa ruka*!' ('Look at the aeroplane') when I saw a bird-cage style lift, peopled by serious matrons, rise steadily in the air!

Until I was in my twenties I really did not feel at home in Australia. And neither, I found, did a great many other Australians. This book shows how they, and I, have fallen in love with this country, how we do feel at home now, how we belong and consider it *ours*.

Obviously, what I write is very much from a South Australian point of view. My life has been so bound up with my own State, and my efforts to achieve improvements for the sake of its people, that I hope readers may excuse what is clearly a regional bias. I love Australia, its vastness, its infinite variety. But I see and enjoy it all from my Australian home in Adelaide.

This scene at Strathalbyn, SA, shows the British influence on Australian building

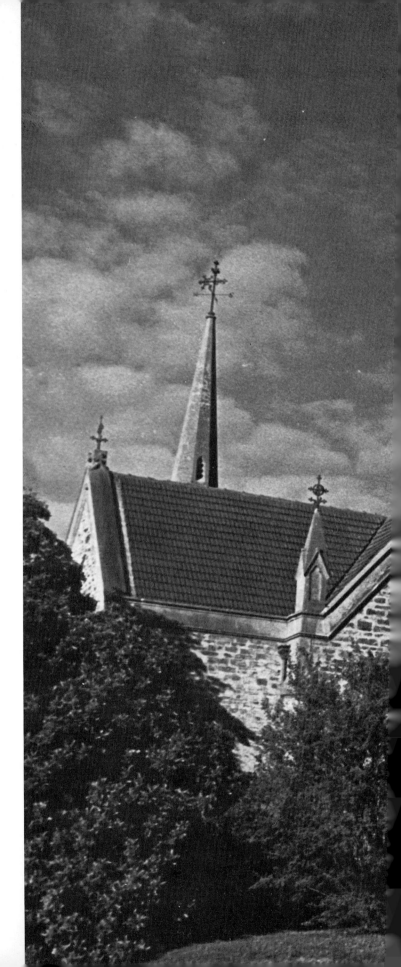

2

Who Loved a Sunburnt Country?

As the first and often unwilling white residents of Terra Australis stepped ashore, they had little realisation of how profoundly the nature of Australia would affect them and their descendants.

They knew they were coming to a very different country from their own, but they viewed that difference through a veil of assumptions which they had grown up with in Europe. These were from an ingrained race-consciousness, developed during 1,400 years of conflict with land and environment from the time of the collapse of the Roman Empire to the end of the eighteenth century.

The misery and squalor of England and Western Europe, from 400 A.D until 800–900 A.D, had demonstrated how long it took for races which had changed their environment (for example the Goths, Visi-Goths, Huns, Slavs, Magyars, Vandals, Saxons, Angles, Jutes and Danes) to adapt to and be at one with their new surroundings.

It was not really until after the Norman conquest of England that the people of that country began to emerge again into a state of settled existence, which used, preserved, and had a sense of oneness with the English environment. After the destruction of previously settled existence in the Roman towns, the despoliation of forests, the wrecking of Celtic culture and countryside,

Anzac marchers reflect Australian pride in the past

Early Sydney folk built homes in European style

and the return of agricultural land to marsh and fen, the miserable hutments in which a small population huddled from hostile weather took centuries to develop into the towns, villages, agriculture, commerce and crafts which emerged in England in the Middle Ages. This progress was accompanied by the sense of pleasure and of being at home in England that was so celebrated by Shakespeare, and to which every Englishman thrilled:—

> *This royal throne of kings, this scept'red*
> *isle,*
> *This earth of majesty, this seat of Mars,*
> *This other Eden, demi-paradise,*
> *This fortress built by Nature for herself*
> *Against infection and the hand of war,*

11

This precious stone set in the silver sea,
Which serves it in the office of a wall,
Or as a moat defensive to a house,
Against the envy of less happier lands,
This blessed plot, this earth, this realm,
  this England . . .

By the nineteenth century this pride of race
was firmly established. Even among those
who were alienated from their own society,
and who were victims of or rejected by their
fellows, there was a sense of identity with the
conditions, outlook and understanding of
their physical and social environment general
in the England of their day. Is it surprising
that Rupert Brooke's most famous poem
should have echoed that view?

  If I should die, think only this of me:
  That there's some corner of a foreign field
  That is for ever England. There shall be
  In that rich earth a richer dust concealed;
  A dust whom England bore, shaped, made
    aware,
  Gave, once, her flowers to love, her ways
    to roam,
  A body of England's, breathing the English
    air,
  Washed by the rivers, blest by the suns of
    home.

But it took centuries of struggle, war,
anguish and agony for that sense to develop.
It has been equally hard for a sense of
oneness with the environment, of race and
cultural identity with place, to begin to
emerge in Australia, a land of such dramatic
contrast with the Europe, and especially the
England, from which the settlers came.

By the first World War, the sense of
personal identification with Australia was
largely chauvinistic—in its true meaning of
'bellicose patriotism'. Australians thought, or
professed to think, that anything Australian
was bigger, better, and more exciting and
remarkable than anything else in the world—
simply because it *was* Australian. By the same
token, Australians were naturally better
sportsmen, horsemen, and all-round
specimens of mankind and womankind than
those of the 'effete Old World'.

In 1891, Rudyard Kipling wrote 'What your
crowd down under are suffering from is
growing pains.' In his *Song of the Cities* he
described Melbourne as 'loud-voiced and
reckless as the wild tide-race / that whips our
harbour-mouth.'

Australian military feats between 1915–18
intensified this chauvinism. Francis Rolland,
chaplain of the 14th Battalion AIF, wrote in
his diary after the Diggers checked the
German assault in 1918: 'I have never seen
our men so irrepressible—bubbling with self-
assurance, confidence, pride in their
achievements . . . Australians were never
modest: they will be insufferable now.'

But chauvinism is an uneasy and self-
defensive emotion. In Australia it was part of
a split personality. On the one hand,
Australians were belligerently proud of their
country. On the other, they were taught that
their heritage was British. England was
commonly referred to as 'Home'. English
history, and English literature, were taught in
schools, and Henry Lawson's 'Wattle and
Waratah' came a bad second to
Wordsworth's daffodils. Australian children
learnt of their glorious heritage, but it was
British, not Australian. It was compounded of
a glamorous mixture of the Thin Red Line,
Trafalgar, Shakespeare, Good Queen Bess,
British justice, Roundheads and Cavaliers
(heavily loaded on the side of King Charles
the Martyr) and traditional Christmas Days in
Charles Dickens style with snowdrifts, holly,
and steaming bowls of punch.

Consequently the average Australian grew
up with an almost reverential attitude
towards Great Britain, but with a contempt
for 'Pommies' because they were not
Australian.

When I was a child in an Australian school,

we were all taught to recite:—

> *I love a sunburnt country*
> *A land of sweeping plains*
> *Of rugged mountain ranges,*
> *Of droughts and flooding rains,*
> *I love her far horizons,*
> *I love her jewel-sea,*
> *Her beauty and her terror,*
> *The wide brown land for me!*

—but we didn't *mean* it. We had been taught also, both in and out of school, that the English countryside is the most beautiful in the world, and so it was difficult both to love a sunburnt country and to pay homage to the rain-drenched beauty of England.

In secondary school we were taught Australian history from a book called *Australia since 1606* by G. V. Portus. (I was later to study history and political science under him at university). By the time a youngster reached high school he was fairly solidly indoctrinated in the history of the British Empire but usually he knew little, and cared less, about the history of his own country. Portus tried to get some flicker of interest in Australian history by *joking* about it.

The problem of identification with the new country took concrete form very early in Australian history. When the settlers built their first permanent homes they paid no attention to local conditions. They built

Tasmanian farmhouse in classic Australian style

Cornish miners brought their building styles to South Australia

replicas of English architecture, developed through the centuries to withstand Northern European and English climate and conditions. In Sydney Town, they built English-style houses and cottages. But all European races brought their own traditions—the German Lutheran refugee settlers in South Australia used the cottage building style of Silesia!

After the convict settlements had been established in New South Wales and Tasmania, Edward Gibbon Wakefield wrote his *Letter from Sydney*. This was to establish the philosophy of settlement in South Australia and profoundly affect that of Western Australia. The whole thesis of his remarkable document was that the physical conditions of life and the social structure in the Australian settlements were not

sufficiently like that best of all possible worlds—England in the 1830s. Therefore, new colonies must be founded in a way that would be more nearly in accord with 'home'. He darkly prophesied that the settlers of New South Wales would grow up to hate the Mother Country more than had those of America, since they would have more opportunity to grow up poor, ignorant, wild and democratical!

This renewed the impetus to export the life of England to a very different territory. The settlements were attempts to create a 'Little England'. As the economy developed on the basis of pastoral and then agricultural pursuits, the classic Australian house emerged. This house had a central core of two or four rooms, divided centrally by a passage. Often, the roof was pitched to continue on beyond the wall line to form a wide verandah all round, or the verandah, on one or more sides of the house, was added later. Kitchen and washhouse, originally in separate buildings at the rear, came to be incorporated in the back verandah, enclosed for the purpose.

This simple structure paid some heed to a climate and lifestyle very different from those of the homeland. In most of Australia it was essential to shelter the outer walls and windows from the fierce heat of the sun, and to provide an airy covered area so that the family might enjoy what we now call 'outdoor living.'

But, to begin with, such homes were limited to those who could not afford anything better. Generally speaking, the wealthy squatters, farmers and pastoralists made little contribution to the development of an indigenous Australian architecture. The Australian countryside is peopled with large houses, such as the manor houses of Tasmania and the great family piles of Riverina and Western Victoria, which are not so large as the great country houses of England but nevertheless are substantial and much larger than those in the mainstream of this nation of house owners. Usually they were no better adapted to the environment than the average Australian suburban home and perhaps less so. Many were adorned with crenellations, as if one might expect to see the inhabitants dodging behind the battlements to repel invaders with bows and arrows.

But the real enemy was the heat, especially in those days of multi-layered clothing, and they dealt with this by providing rooms which were partly underground and were therefore much cooler in the heat of summer than the rest of the house. Old Anlaby, the Dutton family's beautiful old home in South Australia, and Ayers House which is now the Adelaide headquarters of the National Trust of South Australia, each contains a set of underground rooms which were used as retreats in summertime.

Some suburban architecture adopted the same idea, and cellars or underground rooms were important aids to gracious living in the days before refrigeration and air-conditioning. But the cost of excavation and the problem of providing adequate damp protection seem to have discouraged the practice.

Hans Heysen landscape, Adelaide Hills

Early settlers built English-style mansions in Tasmania

15

The one part of Australia where the environment had a long-lasting effect on architecture was Queensland and the tropical north. The heavy summer rainfall and clinging humidity prompted early settlers to raise their timber homes on 'high stumps', six to eight feet high, to lift them above the sodden and sometimes flooded earth and allow free sub-floor ventilation. Many of these homes, unkindly referred to as 'cheeseboxes on stilts', are distinctly unlovely, but some of the older larger homes, with wide verandahs and the stumps enclosed with neatly-painted lattice, have a certain period charm.

Such homes, built in the 'tin and timber' era of tropical architecture, may seem like an attempt to conform with the environment. In fact they were a compromise and, in some places, totally unsuitable. This was exemplified during the 1974 Darwin cyclone,

when modernised versions of the high-stump homes were shattered by the winds. Most of their replacements have been built closer to the ground and to some extent 'cyclone-proofed'.

A prime example of the importation of a building style may be seen in 'Australia's Little Cornwall', in South Australia. Cornish miners emigrated here to work in the copper mines, and very soon they used the local stone to build cottages and chapels which are almost exact replicas of those in their home country except that they have roofs of galvanised iron instead of slate. These buildings have little affinity with the environment.

The attitude of the settlers was not that they should adapt to this strange and possibly hostile environment, but that the environment should somehow adapt itself to them. It was an attitude compounded both of hope and

A fine example of a Queensland 'high-stump' home

ignorance and the common human ability to see what is not there simply because one wants it to be there.

After Eyre had found the vastness, the awesome emptiness, yet spectacular beauty of the Northern Flinders, the people of South Australia decided against all the evidence, and against the warnings of Goyder, that it could be 'civilised' and converted into a great wheatgrowing area. Consequently many foreign maps of Australia carry the name of a non-existent town: Farina. Obviously named as a great wheat centre, in a region where wheat cannot survive, it was planned and laid out but never settled.

My father had reason to know and regret the refusal of South Australian settlers to acknowledge the limitations of their environment. In 1876, land-hungry settlers were allowed to take up land for wheat farming beyond the rainfall line already mapped to define the areas suitable for agriculture. My grandparents were among those who followed them. It was farming in an area unsuitable for the crops they planted. In the early 1890s, bad seasons and a rural depression wiped out many of them. In a fit of depression and fevered with illness my grandfather shot himself and a sad procession of widow and six small children came back to Adelaide to a period of poverty and quite severe privation.

So far as the settlers did appreciate their environment, they still needed to soften, to idealise it. The settlers planted the elms, birches, cedars and oaks of home, rather than the great Australian trees. When those exotics would not grow, they planted pepperinas to shade and soften the angularity and harshness of the landscape.

The first great Australian artist to affect Australians with a love for the Australian landscape—Sir Hans Heysen—nevertheless did so through a cloud of German idealism. It was probably a necessary step to the settlers' feeling at home, that they should see their

Aboriginal child in the Musgrave Ranges

surroundings so romanticised as to appear at home on a myriad local chocolate boxes.

Throughout the first century and a half of Australian settlement the settlers could have learnt many lessons from the indigenous inhabitants—the Aborigines. Over the 50,000 years of their known existence in Australia they had come to identify with their environment to such an extent that they considered themselves physically and spiritually a part of the land—and it of them. The dream-life, the myth, the whole central strength of Aboriginal life dealt with the sacred land.

But the settlers regarded the Aborigines as stone-age primitives, who must be weaned from their heathen ignorance to the enlightened alienation which possessed the white man. Until 1965 the official policy of governments in Australia towards Aborigines was that of 'assimilation'. Most people who gave sincere thought to the plight of the Aborigines, and such people were quite few and far between, believed sincerely that they

should be educated into the same motives, aspirations, modes of life and loyalties as white Australians; to live in the same way and be indistinguishable from them except by colour of skin. Most of the missions to the Aborigines, of all denominations, devoted themselves to this cause. Until the Aborigines could obtain this state of grace they were subject to 'protection'. They were treated as children to be taught but not consorted with, segregated but not befriended. Their persons, property, marriages and children were subject to white management and direction.

Apparently none of the settlers ever paused to wonder how it was that the Aboriginal tribes could lead a complete and satisfying life of the body and spirit, with a complex social structure and a vivid background of ritual and ceremonial, in their harsh environment. The settlers did not even regard them as actual possessors of the land, and solemnly apportioned Australia among themselves without any thought of tribal territories. Very soon, they treated the Aborigines as vermin, to be eradicated as thoroughly as they eradicated dingoes.

The Aborigines' deep instinctive and practical knowledge of Australia could have smoothed the settlers' paths and saved them from many mistakes. Instead, they were treated with ignorance, arrogance and disdain. From the first, the landtakers made no attempt to appreciate that the Aborigines had much to teach, and they were approached with the assumption that man by nature was materialist and attracted to the work ethic. At the first settlement of Sydney it was suggested that the way to improve the lot of these savages was to build a good house for their chief who then, appreciating the benefits of European domestic comfort, would lead his subjects on to work hard to attain them for themselves. No-one bothered to find out that the Aborigines had no 'chief'—that decisions were made by tribal consensus, that materialism was anathema to them, that the

work ethic was so contrary to their outlook that they could understand the motives of the settlers no more than the settlers understood them, and that they found European housing uncomfortable and claustrophobic.

Fortunately for the settlers, the Aboriginal philosophy did not comprehend the waging of war for the sake of territorial gain or military honour. Much of the fighting they did among themselves was of a semi-ritual nature. If Australia had been populated by indigenes such as the Maoris or Fijians, who delighted in war for its own sake and in the case of the Maoris were able to fight British expeditionary forces to a standstill, the subsequent Aboriginal history of Australia might have been very different. Many Aborigines put up a bitter resistance to the invasion of their territories, but their tribal groups were too small and their weapons too primitive to stand against white men on horseback armed with pistols and rifles.

I came to know the Aboriginal people gradually. I suppose it was natural that I should have felt sympathetically towards them. Growing up in Fiji, where the European population was largely Australian, I had been as a child appalled by the race prejudice and colour-bar insistence universally practised by my own kind. I went to a European school, fully staffed by New Zealand trained teachers, for which my parents did not pay fees. The qualification for entry was that you should be at least of majority European descent. No such school was available for the other races—the Fijians and Indians. The latter, indeed, had to raise money for schools as a community effort. We were taught swimming in the Suva baths. It was a segregated pool. No-one with dark skin pigmentation was allowed into the water. The exploitation, social barriers, and affronts to personal pride which the Europeans meted out to the indigenous population aroused my indignation and ire. After graduation I practised law in Fiji, and members of the European Electors

Aboriginal elder at Amata

League suggested that I should stand for the Legislative Council. I had to reply that if I honestly put my view to European electors, they certainly wouldn't elect me. They would more likely tar and feather me and run me out of town.

Fiji, happily, has changed. And so has Australia. But it has been a long, hard fight over these last twenty-five years.

When I first entered Parliament in South Australia, most Aborigines were subject to 'protection'. They could be ordered out of town by a police officer if he thought proper. Unless a board decided to exempt them from protection, they could not own property, have legal custody of their children, contract credit, or drink liquor. Some areas of Crown land were set aside for Aborigines and known as

'reserves', but these could be (and often were) removed from them by Government fiat and without compensation. On these reserves their behaviour was subject to special further regulations not applicable to the rest of the Australian community. The reserve superintendent could censor their mail and hold monies due to them in a trust account which he administered.

The government of the day introduced a further refinement which I fought vehemently but at the time unsuccessfully. They made it an offence for anyone who was not a non-exempt Aborigine to consort with (i.e. keep company with) a non-exempt Aborigine. Ostensibly this move was to protect the 'unsophisticated' Aborigines of the reserves from callous outsiders. In fact it was

bureaucratic paternalism at its worst. Even for an *exempt* Aborigine it was an offence to be seen associating with one of his brothers who had no exemption certificate.

After I had fought and lost that campaign, Aborigines sought more and more to involve me in their struggles for just and fair treatment. I was the last non-Aborigine to be president of the Federal Council for the Advancement of Aborigines and Torres Strait Islanders.

Eventually we made a tremendous breakthrough. South Australia, while I was Minister for Aboriginal Affairs, swept away all laws and regulations which discriminated against Aborigines, including the hated 'protection' system. We set up the first Aboriginal Lands Trust to give land rights to Aborigines, and passed the first Act in Australia to make it an offence to discriminate against anyone on the grounds of race, colour of skin or country of origin.

Concurrently, there was a fight to change the Australian immigration policy. This again was stupidly racist, and based on maintenance of the antique White Australia policy. Within the Labor Party my support for reform of that policy led to a bitter personal breach with my friend Arthur Calwell. Removal of the White Australia plank from the Labor Party platform took years of struggle which culminated in complete victory in the Federal Conference of the Labor Party in Launceston in 1972. This was followed by the carrying into effect of a non-racial immigration policy by Labor's first Minister in that portfolio in the Whitlam Labor Government, Al Grassby.

The change in the laws did not, of course, automatically bring about a change in community and social attitudes. But, as white Australians came into social contact with more and more people of races and skin colours different from their own, tolerance

Sir Douglas Nicholls, first Aboriginal governor of an Australian State, at the swearing-in ceremony. Don Dunstan is at the microphone

and liking grew and prejudices fell away. The
stranger is no longer regarded as necessarily
inferior and hostile. The change in the degree
of evidence of racial prejudice is very marked.

In 1953, when I was first in Parliament, my
opponents thought it was electorally
advantageous to spread the myth that I was
not of Australian descent at all. They used
the fact that I was born in Fiji for the basis of
a whispering campaign, to the effect that I
was a 'Melanesian or plain half-caste
bastard'. This rumour gained wide
circulation. The point was that they thought
it was something which would *discredit* me.
Nowadays most people would say 'So what?'
In 1976 I married a lady of Chinese descent,
and the public reaction is not the hostility
which would have been evident twenty-five
years ago, but envy (which is justified).

There is still a long way to go. True, our
immigration officials no longer scour Europe
for light-skinned, non-English speaking
migrants (whose social customs will make
their integration to Australia painful), because
their skin colour will give a suitable reaction
to a light meter, while excluding an English-
speaking fully-qualified medico from Hong
Kong. But in 1977 it was still chalked up as a
record for a full-blood Aboriginal to gain
entry to a Northern Territory RSL Club while
in my company—an Aboriginal veteran of
Vietnam having been *refused* entry to that
same Club.

The balance of public opinion in the large
cities, however, is now emotionally as well as
intellectually against race prejudice and in
favour of treating people as human beings.
Yet we still have not begun to learn lessons
from the Aborigines which are there for the
asking. Doug Nicholls, my old friend of those
battles for the Aboriginal rights, could
become the Aboriginal governor of an
Australian State, and was received with warm
public acclaim, but his proud tribal fellow-
Aborigines of the Musgrave Ranges live
beyond the ken of most Australians.

One of the barriers to understanding lies in racial attitudes to the soil. There is a strange ambivalence about this. The Japanese, for example, are among the world's most meticulous gardeners and intense agriculturists, and they use every scrap of soil on their rocky islands. Yet they are fanatical about cleansing their skins from the least stain of the earth they cherish. Maybe this is because of the centuries in which they used human excrement as a soil fertiliser. Australians probably rank about next in this fanatical desire to cleanse one's skin from the soil. As we shall see, Australians follow the English tradition in that we are a nation of gardeners, but we are all careful to scrub away any traces of the soil. Even in our language, soil is a synonym for dirt. To be uncleaned of earth is to be sleazy and unhygienic.

The tribal Aboriginal, however, regards the soil as his element. It is the sacred land. He is not merely on it or in it, but *of* it. When Aborigines in the tribal areas appear publicly they are most likely to carry traces of earth on their skins somewhere, and in their culture that is not only hygienic but *clean*. This difference in outlook is a real barrier to white Australian understanding of the Aborigines. It is one of the reasons why we have not appreciated or developed their food resources for ourselves. White Australians joke about Aborigine's food and sneer at witchetty grubs, snake and goanna. They shouldn't.

Let me tell you a story. When I first went to Amata, in the North West Aboriginal Reserve in South Australia in 1965, I met a fascinating Aborigine woman called Nullinja. In this remote tribal location there was no State school. The elders petitioned me for one, but in the meantime had started a school of their own. All the small children crowded into an old shed where Nullinja presided. She was a born teacher, and fascinating to watch. She

Nullinja interprets 'white man's news' to her people

remained a great force for good in her own community. The school books were clean. All the children (and Nullinja) lived in the traditional wiltjas—wind breaks sheltering a fire. No doubt as part of their keen sense of fun and the absurd, they nudged one of the older boys to read from one of the ancient 'readers' for school children which they had managed to acquire from a mission. He read, 'I must keep healthy. I must get plenty of fresh air. I must always leave my window open at night.'

Recently, revisiting the reserve, I found I was to be treated to an inma: a feast with entertainment. We sat on the earth round cooking fires while Nullinja pounded the wild grain they had collected to make a coarse flour for genuine damper. Cooked in the coals, it was delicious, like a flavoursome oatmeal cookie. Then came a kangaroo cooked in its skin. They gave me a piece of the tail, which was succulent and excellent. Then, as relish, there was a bowl of honey ants. If you have never tasted these you have missed a treat. The ants carry honey in a fine bulbous membrane about the size of one's little finger nail. You pick up the tiny body of the ant, put the membrane in your mouth and suck. You get a draught of pure fresh honey, the best I've ever tasted. Then there was a dish of native wild tomatoes. Fresh, these have an excellent tart astringency of the quality of a good olive: a taste like a cross between a ripe olive and guava. Going dry they have a raisin-like taste which is very pleasant. Afterwards, as her friends chanted, Nullinja, now painted, danced one of the woman's dances. Everyone had great fun.

But how many Australians of the past even tried to enrich their lives and taste experiences with what was here for so long before they came? For those who have succeeded them, it is almost too late. Aboriginal communities in the settled areas

have long since been destroyed, degraded, or driven away. Those in the far outback are rarely seen by the average white Australian, and in any case they are by this time so rightly suspicious of outsiders, or so deeply involved in complex problems introduced by white men, that it is next to impossible to participate in their way of life.

The point is that, if the earliest settlers had not been so arrogantly confident that it was only *their* lifestyle which was worthy of consideration, and that it must be imposed upon the Australian environment at all costs,

Homeward-bound after a food-gathering expedition

24

there might have been some basis for co-existence.

Instead, the battle was won by the men with the guns. A unique lifestyle, developed over 500 centuries, was almost obliterated in about fifty years. And the irony is that many people now seek the wilderness in order to escape from the ratrace of the cities . . . but they take the ratrace with them as they gallivant over the landscape in four-wheel-drive vehicles. How can they ever rediscover

Aboriginal woman from Amata

Gathering wild tomatoes

the serenity, the interwoven closeness with the land, destroyed by their forefathers?

Of course the Australians were not the only people to degrade an indigenous population. The Americans did the same thing, but nevertheless they seemed to come to terms with the new environment more rapidly than did the Australians. Only one example is that of eating habits. Apart from such things as potatoes and sweet corn, which spread quickly around the world, the Americans adapted to such exotic foods as catfish, squirrel, possum, buffalo, terrapin, and bear. In Australia, a few early eccentrics told of the joys of eating echidna and some settlers relished 'Pom Jam' (roast kangaroo tail) and 'Slippery Bob' (kangaroo brains cooked in corn oil) but most people regarded Australian fauna and flora as alien and undesirable food sources.

But something like 300,000 Aborigines were living prosperously on Australian food resources when white men invaded the continent. According to the *Australian*

Encyclopaedia, they enjoyed a rich variety of plant and animal foods. They knew more than 200 food plants and many different species of birds, mammals, fishes, eggs, reptiles, amphibians, shellfish and molluscs.

Furthermore they had developed specific methods of cooking each delicacy and even of food preservation. The conventional picture of Aboriginal cooking is of half-raw kangaroo, and seeds plucked by nomads and ground into nardoo. In fact they enjoyed such dishes as bulrush roots steam-cooked for several days, dampers made of dried and pulverised cycad palm nuts, and conserved quandongs. They knew how to preserve food by drying and other methods and they feasted on various delicacies as they came into season.

But, in this land of plenty, the guards and convicts of the First Fleet almost starved because they were running short of salt pork and hard biscuit. They were so reluctant to eat local food that Governor Phillip had to issue rations of six pounds of fresh locally-caught fish instead of one pound of salt pork that may have been several years in its cask.

Facing page: Playtime at Amata
Dinnertime at Amata. Cutting up a kangaroo

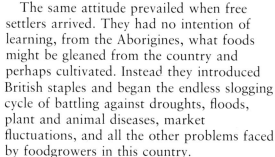

The same attitude prevailed when free settlers arrived. They had no intention of learning, from the Aborigines, what foods might be gleaned from the country and perhaps cultivated. Instead they introduced British staples and began the endless slogging cycle of battling against droughts, floods, plant and animal diseases, market fluctuations, and all the other problems faced by foodgrowers in this country.

The point is that the settlers regarded the natural flora and fauna as alien, and therefore unacceptable. They must be dismissed from the environment and replaced by those with which the settlers were familiar. No one would eat plump young kangaroo while even the oldest, toughest sheep still remained to be slaughtered.

The kangaroo became our national emblem, but it was still alien in spirit to white Australians either of the city or the country. I remember David Gulpilil, the superb Aboriginal actor and dancer, saying to me with glee 'You Europeans talk of being descended from monkeys. But there were no monkeys in Australia. I think we Aborigines are descended from reptiles.'

To David, being at one in spirit with Australian reptiles was natural and joyful, in a way that cannot be dreamed of by any descendant of Australia's white settlers.

Bush tucker at Amata

Witchetty grub

Facing page: Looking for honey ants

3

Material Triumph, Aesthetic Disaster

Most Australians, then, grew up without a real sense of identity with the Australian environment. Sure, they looked on the place where they had grown up as home, be it never so humble, and Australia was 'good old Aus'. But they had not developed the same kind of identity with the land as that which was part of the personalities of Englishmen, New England settlers, or Europeans. Many fifth generation Australians looked upon England, and indeed referred to it, as the 'Mother Country'. Their hearts were still divided between this faraway motherland, which in the days before jet aircraft was unattainable by most Australians, and their pride in their true homeland.

This situation was compounded by the modern malaise of city life. Australia has become the most urban nation in the world. A higher proportion of Australians live in the capital cities and larger towns than is the case with any other race or group on earth, and although one may feel links with a street or a suburb this is vastly different from the interlocking of spirit between a people and a land.

In searching for identity with Australia, it was inevitable that Australians should develop their own symbol—the typical or archetypal Aussie.

This was the sun-bronzed man of the

The 'symbolic' Australian does exist . . . but there are not many left

outback who had conquered the Australian harshness; broken the back of the hostile environment. In the Australian ethos, this rugged individualist is the folk hero. He has been represented countless times in books and on film, and for many years the actor Chips Rafferty was seen as his incarnation. (Which is rather ironical because Rafferty, whose real name was Goffage, originally wanted to be an artist: a profession definitely not in tune with the outback image). However Chips Rafferty did symbolise the man whom we thought of

Mustering cattle by helicopter, northern Western Australia

31

as distinctively Australian: a bronzed centaur of the wide open spaces and definitely not a dweller in the suburbs.

The legend has persisted so strongly that the first feature film made by the South Australian Film Corporation (an organisation which has so profoundly affected the recent development of the Australian film industry that other States are hastening to try to copy it) was *Sunday Too Far Away*, starring Jack Thompson as a gun-shearer.

The whole myth ignores the fact that the rural population of Australia is falling steadily. The 1966 census showed that 83.19 per cent of Australians lived in urban areas and 16.62 per cent in the country. By 1971 these proportions had changed to 85.57 and 14.29, at a time when the population increased by more than a million, and the imbalance has continued ever since. Even thirty years ago the grazing industry employed only 95,270 people out of a total working population, in 1947, of 3.20 million.

Moreover, the typical rural dweller in Australia is rarely to be seen droving or yarning with his mates over a camp fire, swilling strong tea from his billy-can and eating damper. These days about the only white Australians to cook damper are fledgling Boy Scouts for whom it is regarded as part of 'great adventure'! The real picture of Australian inland folk is quite different. Station owners muster their cattle with helicopters, and use their own light aircraft for trips to town. The jackaroo does his work on a motorbike instead of a horse. The drover follows the cattle in a Range Rover, towing a caravan equipped with all mod cons. The wheat farmer sits in a sophisticated, air-conditioned header, the fruit farmer in a motorised buggy. The grape farmer is buying automatic pickers, and farmers' houses are usually equipped with modern conveniences.

But the average Australian lives in suburbia. City centres in this country never developed the high population densities of European and American cities, where town houses and apartment blocks rise amid stores and office buildings. In Australia, the spread of suburbia has been more rapid and extensive than elsewhere.

The Australian, like his English forebears, loves his garden. (22 million Englishmen are reputed to claim gardening as their sole hobby). It is a natural and creative urge to want to have some relationship with the soil, not only to watch but to help to make plants grow. In West Berlin and in Warsaw, on both sides of the Iron Curtain, inhabitants cooped up in the little boxes of high-rise apartments queue for the right to use a little plot of earth, a few feet square, some distance from their apartment, to grow a few vegetables and flowers. In Australia it is normal for millions of people to take that privilege for granted, and to enjoy a plot of land which by European standards is incredibly generous. Most Australians would not stand for the claustrophobia of high density high-rise cities, although some people, especially in Sydney and Melbourne, have been forced into high-rise living under schemes to rehouse families living in

Facing page: High-rise housing, Redfern, Sydney
Night scene, Canberra

substandard accommodation. Such schemes have introduced to Australia all the problems of high-rise living which were defined overseas as long as twenty years ago. In Australia, the centres of cities are rapidly denuded of population after working hours, except for significant areas of urban blight, and everyone speeds home to his or her segment of the suburbs.

But the suburbs themselves have been a rejection of the Australian environment. The typical Australian suburb was constituted by quarter-acre blocks. On these were built single family homes. Usually set uniformly twenty-five feet from the street frontage, they put their best face to the front. Often it was a deliberately false façade: an obligatory method of keeping up with the Joneses. The twenty-five feet were occupied by the front garden—not a place for privacy or enjoyment, but a show for the neighbours and passers-by. (How often do you see a family sitting in their *front* garden?) The front room of the house was usually the parlor, containing the best furniture and glass-fronted cabinets of imported china and bric-a-brac. It was rarely used. At the rear of the house was the kitchen

Suburban sprawl, Adelaide

and sometimes the diningroom—the most lived-in rooms in the house. These gave onto the back garden, the only place where the family enjoyed the benefits of the Australian climate. It contained the clothes-line, a rainwater tank. an incinerator, maybe a barbecue and vegetable patch. It never seemed to strike suburban dwellers that by building English-style cottages in Australian suburbs they were depriving themselves of the best advantages of Australian conditions, circumscribing the privacy they wanted with ugliness, and living in houses which were too hot in summer and too cold in winter. Robin Boyd, in writing the story of an Australian home, said 'This is the story of a material triumph and an aesthetic disaster.' Certainly we have—or at least most of us have— escaped the British and European horror: highrise high density boxes in which people live as unnaturally as hens in a battery. The question remains as to how much better what we *have* is than what we have *escaped*. The average Australian suburb, mile upon mile of houses each reflecting infinite variations upon the basic formula of five rooms, kitchen, and bath, is too often an aesthetic disaster. And, of course, formula homes create formula living, and programme their occupants into an almost unbreakable lifestyle. It is snug and comfortable enough, but unadventurous and stultifying. When Barry Humphries created Edna Everage, and made Australia laugh at itself and Sandy Stonesville, his satire (like all true satire) was based upon the truth long known to everyone but ignored by common consent.

However there have been attempts to break out of the suburban syndrome. The first of the major governmental housing schemes was in the 1920s: the 'Thousand Homes Scheme' of the South Australian Labor Government of that time. Named Colonel Light Gardens after the founder-planner of Adelaide, it was

Facing page: The 'Versailles concept', Canberra. The Australian War Memorial faces Parliament House (top)

landscaped more deliberately than any other suburb and planned with tree-lined streets, the occasional neighbourhood park, and a street layout which cut down on fast through traffic. But it was no more Australian than any other suburb. Each of its bungalows was built to the familiar formula and it was utterly divorced from the environment. It merely had a bigger 'nature strip' planted with non-Australian trees.

Canberra, of course, is the prime example of Australian city-planning. However it was not planned as an essentially *Australian* city, but rather as a Versailles in the Australian bush. It is interesting that King O'Malley, the Minister responsible for the board which adjudicated on the international design competition for the city, was Canadian-born. The first, second, and third prizes went to Walter Burley Griffin, an American; Eliel Saarinen, a Finn; and the Frenchman D. A. Agache. Apparently none of the prizewinners ever saw the site before drawing their plans. When Griffin came to Australia to supervise construction, he soon fell out with Prime Minister Billy Hughes, a Welshman.

Predictably, the design pays no heed to the 'Australianness' of its location and environment. In fact Griffin's plan has compounded the social stratification inevitable in a city to be populated by a public service hierarchy, and social isolation is even more rigidly defined by spaces and distances which demand motor transport. Canberra has a higher motor-car population than the rest of Australia and even the USA. Just ponder these figures. At last count, the USA had 438 sedans and station-wagons for every 1,000 people, Australia as a whole 354, South Australia 378, and Canberra 439.

The phenomenon of personal isolation — from one's neighbours and neighbourhood and from cohesive social groupings — which is such a feature of modern urban life, is therefore exaggerated in Canberra. Many residents grope for words in attempts to

36

describe the atmosphere of the city and usually conclude 'Cold . . . soul-less.' There is an alienation of house from house, house from neighbourhood, house from relevance to the city as a whole.

And this is a pity because Canberra has such great potential beauty. But something is lacking. The city is like a woman expensively coiffured, dressed, and made-up, well-educated, courteous—and frigid. Canberra boasts more than a million trees and shrubs, but many are exotics and most are neatly regimented. Pretty, but it could be a city of anywhere. When you sit up in the Lakeside Hotel and look out at the nightscape, the only thing seemingly missing is Flash Gordon whizzing around the curve below. But what is *really* missing is any feeling of Australia.

Other Australian cities have suffered all the problems of cities elsewhere in the twentieth century. As the suburbs have sprawled further and further afield, exhausting their inhabitants with long trips in to work and back and making them less willing to return to the city in the evenings, so the city centres became dead hearts. Now, they are mostly shopping and business areas without residential components, and in consequence empty and lifeless at times available for leisure and socialising. Boyd remarked, of Adelaide's tendency to this condition: 'You won't have a city and suburbs—for soon there won't be an urb to be sub.' After 5.30 p.m. the city population returns to the dormitory areas in which they have their homes. These sprawl in ugly low density streetscapes, and for the most part without the planning or the social amenities to form the great conurbations of Australia.

In these homes, Australians tend not only to be isolated from the natural environment of Australia but from one another. They 'keep themselves to themselves'. The suburbs provide few means of meaningful human

The daily invasion from suburbia, Melbourne

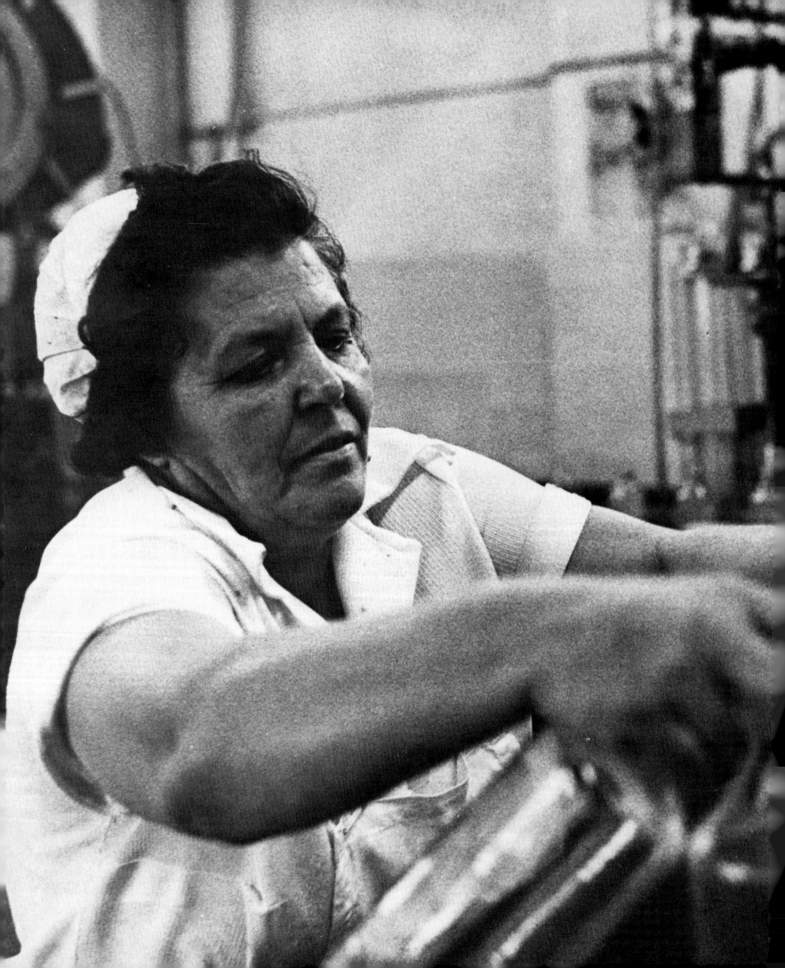

association. Neighbours know little of one another. Few can tell you the names of other people in their street, let alone know these people as friends. No more than a quarter of suburban populations are members of groups and associations. Transport also tends to isolate people, whether they use private cars, trains, trams, or buses. In Sydney and Melbourne, an average of two hours a day is spent in commuting to the workplace and back, adding up to years of isolation in each working citizen's life.

The workplace, too, in large factories or workshops, in process work or office, tends to isolate and alienate. There is little opportunity for group interaction on the production line.

There is a theory that a number of strikes are prompted not by actual discontent with working conditions, but rather that the strike, when it occurs, is an eruption of deeper frustrations: an attempt to break the deadlock of routine, itself a cause of isolation, and join one's workmates in an activity which gives some prospect of creative satisfaction. If you can join with your acquaintances in forcing the employer to give you something, it is more likely to be satisfying than obeying the orders of a foreman—or worse still, of a computer.

Isolation, alienation, tend inevitably to break down the social reinforcement of strength and integration of personality. The norms of behaviour are less appreciated as the outcome of group pragmatism. In plain words, the fabric of social life tends to decay. As a direct consequence, there is an increase in mental illness, crime, family stress and juvenile delinquency.

This happens in all large modern cities. But in Australia the problem is compounded by alienation from the countryside, the essentially Australian environment.

On the production line in a Sydney factory

4

Marooned in Suburbia

The most significant features of the social life of Australian suburbs are those associated with sport, with public houses and clubs, and to a lesser extent with membership of churches and minor local associations.

Traditionally, there are three kinds of involvement in sport. The first is personal involvement in team sports, engaged in by a fairly small section of the populace after leaving school. The second comprises the 'social sports' such as tennis, golf, yachting, squash, and so on, in which opportunities for socialising are as important as the sport itself. The third and most important is spectator involvement in Australia's major 'blood sports'.

Our climate and terrain allow us to organise a wide range of sporting activities in a way which is, by any international comparison, relatively inexpensive. In Britain, a man with the urge to shoot birds or beasts is obliged to pay hundreds of guineas to join a syndicate which rents a 'shoot' from its owners. In Japan, our major trading partner, a game of golf is likely to cost $75. Many Japanese, unable to commute to a golf club or afford membership fees, may be seen standing on a great tiered scaffold, driving ball after ball into a large net. In Australia, a game on a good public course will cost you only a few dollars.

Australian Rules spectators

Port Adelaide barrackers

But sport affects the largest groups of the populace by providing a spectacle—a stimulus of excitement sometimes added to by gambling.

Outstanding amongst these sports is Australian Rules Football, the game peculiar to Victoria, South Australia, Western Australia, and Tasmania. Fast moving, spectacular and rough, it allows spectators an outlet for aggression, coupled with parochial loyalty. It regularly attracts crowds of tens of thousands, to watch players who are professionals or semi-professionals and who endeavour to gain membership of and selection by the team which offers the highest material rewards. Identification with these teams of gladiators goes far beyond those who are in any way active socially in the

41

football clubs, and conversation about football forms the easiest basis of social communication amongst the otherwise isolated residents of suburbia. Indeed, for many Australians, identification with the team is the one obvious activity in which they can feel a release from social isolation. Without involvement in group activity, with few meaningful social contacts in the suburb or at work, team support can give a real sense of 'belonging' which is otherwise missing.

Rather similar comments might apply to cricket, especially Test cricket. In this game, spectator involvement becomes more national and less parochial, and sometimes approaches chauvinism.

Punters at Labor Day race meeting, Morphettville, SA

To a lesser extent, Rugby League in New South Wales and Queensland, and soccer among post-war migrants all over the country, fulfil a similar role.

The other major spectator sports—horseracing, trotting, greyhound racing—do not provide the same outlets for aggression and team identification. Instead, they substitute associated gambling to ensure adequate excitement and attraction. They also attract large crowds of regular spectators, even fewer of whom are in any way actively associated with the club organisation responsible for the sport.

The significant feature of these spectator sports is that they provide no effective means of group interaction. They are outlets for people who can get their kicks while anonymous members of a crowd. Personal participation by effective social intercourse with their fellows is largely absent. The spectator sports often (though not, admittedly, for all) can reinforce the isolation of suburbia.

What other opportunities are there in suburbia for socialising with others? While people still bought their goods at their neighbourhood small shops there was an opportunity for social interchange. But the small neighbourhood shops have disappeared. The economics of scale in selling food and household requirements have brought the ubiquitous supermarkets, temples to the anonymous and impersonal. Once, I bought my groceries just round the corner from Mr Gluyas. He knew the wants of his every customer, recommended interesting new lines and carried on a running conversation with everyone in the shop. Today, he and his shop have gone, and I must drive to a supermarket where I push a trolley round a vast series of shelves anxiously searching for the goods on my list. You don't get much social interaction from a twenty-foot shelf of laundry detergent.

In the last century, church life provided a focus for social activity in the suburbs, even though it was also divisive because of the number of denominations which were at best suspicious and at worst hostile.

Recently, most of the hostility has disappeared and ecumenical togetherness has

Barrackers on The Hill, Sydney Cricket Ground

become more evident, but such changes have occurred almost too late. We are in a time of rapidly falling active church membership. The older suburbs, and even some country towns, have a remarkable number of old churches which have fallen into disuse, or have been converted for other purposes, from kindergartens to light industries. In Adelaide, once known as 'the city of churches', one is now being used as a photographer's studio, another as a print shop, and so on. It is rather pathetic when one considers the work, faith, and sacrifice that went into these solid old buildings. In the newer suburbs, there is a much smaller proportion of church building than used to occur. The figures for active church membership are revealing. In a 1974 survey, forty-eight per cent of those interviewed had not attended church within the previous year, and only thirty-three per cent within the previous month. Only twenty-two per cent of Australians were regular churchgoers.

It is apparent that the average Australian, even if he pays lip service to church membership, reserves it for such occasions as weddings, christenings, and funerals. A certain number, of course, do treat the church as a centre of community organisation and social intercourse. Australians of the Greek Orthodox Church are notable among these.

At the other extreme there is pub life, which has not developed in the English style. Perhaps it could have done, but in past decades the Australian pub was subject to prolonged attacks by church and temperance groups and licensing authorities. In New South Wales alone, twenty-seven different Acts to regulate the Liquor trade were passed between 1825 and 1883, and there were three local option polls in the early 1900s. In 1915 and 1916, pubs were obliged to close at six p.m. as a 'wartime measure', but this restriction continued well after the second

Stark supermarket aisles contrast with the friendly 'corner store'

44

World War. In Canberra and the rest of the Australian Capital Territory, liquor sales were totally forbidden until 1928.

In such a climate, the Australian drinker became a guilt-ridden object and the pubs, enchained by a myriad regulations, became joyless oases where the sexes were segregated and entertainments forbidden. No wonder they concentrated upon selling the maximum amount of liquor in the minimum possible time—especially during the 'six o'clock swill'. There was no way they could develop into neighbourhood community centres where a man and his wife and friends could enjoy unbibulous social contacts.

The reforms in Australian licensing laws during the 1960s and 1970s have improved this situation markedly. The 'bloodhouses' are fewer, comfort and service have improved, the sexes are no longer segregated. But the old attitudes linger on. There is still a faint flavour of disgrace about pub life. In the suburban wastelands, pubs tend to remain rather impersonal watering holes.

Club life in Australia is of small significance, except in New South Wales. In that State, mammoth and wealthy club organisations have been founded upon the revenue they derive from poker machines. They provide their members with good and cheap food, quite good entertainment, group tours and outings and a degree of social interaction which appears real. However, many of them are so large that they easily become impersonal.

Outside New South Wales, club life varies enormously according to the age, tradition and social makeup of the suburb. In a few there are clubs and community organisations which really do penetrate and support the community well. But in great areas of the suburbs there is nothing of the kind. In recent times the growth of clubs founded by ethnic minorities of the post-war migration boom is of growing significance, as we shall see.

On the face of it, a list of local

organisations in any suburb looks impressive. Sporting clubs, churches, Mothers and Babies, District Nurse, Meals on Wheels, Senior Citizens, Brass Band, Marching Girls, Boy Scouts, Girl Guides, Friendly Societies, Junior Chamber of Commerce, Service Clubs such as Rotary, Apex and Lions would make it seem as if there were a very lively community life. But any politician worth his salt who has doorknocked his area and got to know residents is forced to the conclusion that local organisations actively include no more than a quarter of the population.

In low density suburbia, the spectacular growth of private car ownership has been inevitable. Public transport cannot economically provide a service which competes on the grounds of economy and convenience. Hence, the cities provided much work for the traffic engineers in the 1960s. No Australian cities had been built to take the projected high traffic densities. The building of freeways, which wrecked and divided suburbs and despoiled the skyline, became of higher and higher priority for the three larger metropolises.

In Adelaide, as part of the studies emanating from the 1962 development plan, we were finally presented with a fat document called 'The Metropolitan Adelaide

Facing page: The 'cook-it-yourself' barbecue in the British Hotel, North Adelaide, typifies the new freedom in Australian pub life. *Below:* Poker machine players, Sydney

Transportation Study'. It was a horror. Great swathes were to be cut for freeways through suburbia: north, south, east, west and sideways. A great slice of northern parklands was to disappear under a giant 'traffic exchange'. I was Leader of the Opposition at the time, and as soon as possible after studying the MATS Plan I took off to the USA and Europe to look at some experiences in this area. The consultants who had prepared the study came from the USA and were well known. From Los Angeles to Boston, San Francisco to Atlanta, London to Munich, civic leaders took a look at the proposals and said 'For God's sake, don't do it!'

I didn't take much persuading after I had seen the American experience, including those towering freeways which went nowhere—just stopped in midair when the local citizens, desperate to save their cities from being consumed by the ravenous automobile, refused the necessary bond issues to pay for them. The lesson was clear. It is better to subject the motorist to some inconvenience in intra-city transport than allow his motorcar, which multiplies by the roads it feeds on, to wreck the quality of life of the city's residents.

We saved Adelaide from the awful fate which befell so many American cities. The MATS Plan was scrapped, Adelaide's arterial road system upgraded, and Adelaide remains the gracious city that it has always been.

There are two other features of Australian motor mania. One is that it has significantly increased suburban isolation. When the average suburban person went regularly by bus or tram to work there was a fair chance of his having some regular contact with his neighbours who did the same. But with each citizen commuting, one person to a car, his only communication is with his radio.

The other feature, however, is that more

Democracy in the Domain, Sydney

and more people have been able to get out into the countryside, for recreation and to explore the vastness and beauty of Australia. In the 1950s I remember Howell Witt, the Englishman who is now Anglican Bishop of the North West, saying at a synod meeting to Dr Robin, another Englishman who was then Bishop of Adelaide, 'We hear about the vast open spaces of Australia, but it's only New Australians like you and me, my Lord, who travel them. The Australians stay at home.' Not any more they don't. By car and caravan, Australians have trekked all over their country, and now use four-wheel-drive vehicles to penetrate areas once almost unknown. On every weekend and every holiday there is a great exodus from the cities. I hear complaints that we have no Hyde Park corner in Adelaide; no speakers' centre where people may go to hear

The domination of technology. The eastern suburbs railway overpass swoops over old buildings at Woolloomooloo

49

The new freedom: nudist families on Maslins Beach, SA

those who would harangue them on all manner of topics. We do have one, in Botanic Park, and I used to be required by the Labor Party to speak there. But no-one speaks there any more because no-one comes to listen. They are all off wheeling about to extra-city destinations to fish, swim, explore, barbecue or just look.

As Australian suburbia entered the 1970s, it seemed ripe for deterioration into what Karl Mannheim and others have called *Admass*: a society made up of isolated individuals, each one of an anonymous throng engaged on repetitive work; subject to mass entertainment such as spectator sport or TV, again as an anonymous unit; and cut off from social inter-action with his or her fellows.

In such a situation, the human personality is deprived of the essential nourishment which comes only from close human relationships. Through sheer stress of alienation or isolation, men and women fall prey to all the ills of modern city life.

Fortunately the 'anonymous Australian' shows encouraging signs of breaking out of this pattern and developing a more individualistic lifestyle.

Facing page: The outdoors Australians: sailboats on the Swan River estuary, Perth

50

5

Revolt of the Long Hairs

Anyone involved in the political life of modern democracies must say that their most striking feature is the way in which public opinion, fashion, and motive are constantly dynamic. The winds of change are constantly blowing. They are unpredictable, but it is vital to divine their direction and their changes of direction. Between 1967 and 1977 a great gust of change blew up and to some extent died away. But permanent and lasting results occurred and one of these may be seen in the groves of Academe.

For most of Australia's existence, the life of the universities and institutions of tertiary education had little effect on the political and social consciousness of the population as a whole. For the most part, students in them came from the middle classes, and were, on the whole, conservative.

People outside the universities gave little thought to their existence except on 'rag days' or on the rare occasions when opinions expressed by some group of student radicals made the headlines—such as the famous resolution 'This house will not fight for King and Country' moved by the Oxford Union Debating Society in 1937. Such reports made the average man feel that institutes of learning were hotbeds of sedition. Nothing could have been further from the truth. The majority of university staff (certainly the

A lonely figure at Monash University, Melbourne, seems to symbolise individualism braving the establishment

majority outside the Humanities) and of students were conservative in outlook and support. The radicals were a sometimes active but always beleaguered and small minority.

In the 1950s the general tenor of student activity was career-oriented. Few students would make political commitments or feel that they had any public role or mission. I know. It was my job to organise for the Labor Party in Adelaide University and I didn't do very well.

In 1967, as Premier of South Australia, I went to Adelaide University to address the students. It was apparent that a large proportion of the audience still regarded me as a dangerous revolutionary, even though the university population had greatly increased, and was now drawn from a much wider variety of backgrounds than ever before, because of the government grants which covered tuition and subsistence.

By 1971 the mood at that university and most others in western democracies had completely changed. The questioning of the values of existing society, arising largely from the younger generation's revulsion over the Vietnam involvement, was examining and challenging every tenet of belief. It deeply affected even those from conservative homes and caused great alarm and despondency among the older generation.

In that year, when I was again about to address students at Adelaide University, I was

53

warned by some sympathetic staff members that I should not do so because my safety could not be guaranteed. I was now regarded as too conservative!

On the day of my address, left-wing students with loudhailers urged cheering students to come to see the demise of Dunstan. It was a lively meeting, in which I managed to hold my own, and as I live on to this day the demise, obviously, failed to occur. The radical students had not done their homework, but the interesting and indeed the heartening thing about the whole exercise was that so large a group had been brought to a pitch of commitment to questioning the society in which they lived, and searching for answers to their questions.

After a few years, widespread student radicalism sputtered and died away. The committed and involved radicals are once more a minority. Only a manic few still see me as a conservative ogre. But, for the first time in Australia's history, widespread radicalism of the young affected the whole of society. It has often done so in other countries and at other times, but this was the only time in Australia. It has had a permanent and beneficial effect.

Ironically, however, it was not a purely Australian movement. It was a local manifestation of the American 'student revolt' of the 1960s, which made itself known all over the democratic world in many ways from the turgid work of Herbert Marcuse to the protest songs of Bob Dylan and Joan Baez. Like every human activity it has been an inextricable tangle of good and bad, and it has been exploited in many ways and by many people from drug pushers to department stores, but on the whole it gave young people the belief that there was a cause of good to fight for—the cause of humanity and kindness in which the enemy was crass materialism, the excesses of capitalism, the

Street theatre by university students

54

humbug of the 'establishment', the exploitation of man and the world's resources by unscrupulous and manipulative multinational companies.

All these could be epitomised in the immorality of American and Australian involvement in the Vietnam war. This provided the 'student revolutionaries' with a single banner to march under and they were joined by countless people from every walk of life. All that was happening in the universities began to pervade the entire community and to cause enormous changes in the lifestyle of the Western world, ranging from the revolution in clothing and hairstyling to the profound upheaval of Women's Lib.

As recently as the 1960s the average Australian was locked into a ritual pattern where clothing was concerned. He wore a suit and hat to business and his casual wear, such as it was, was modest and restrained. Hairstyling for men was unheard of. There was only the short back and sides, and most men were terrified of appearing 'pansified'.

Quite suddenly, all that changed. People dared to wear shorts to work, to leave off hats and ties, to wear long hair and beards and attend formal occasions in kaftans or jeans. Old taboos vanished amid cries of doom from the conservatives, and the whole effect has been mentally and physically liberating.

Women's Lib, of course, is a much more serious matter, though it has some link with the clothing revolution. (Ten years ago, a girl office employee would never have gone to work in jeans). For countless Australian women, the work of 'Women's Libbers' who were condemned as cranks and perverts when they first raised their banners on campus has been a literal casting-off of chains. There is still much to be done, but the woman of today enjoys a freedom over her own body and of speech, employment, social mobility and emotional connections that would have horrified society a generation ago.

All these things, which originated in the universities and included the general questioning of accepted patterns of behaviour, jogged suburban isolation and complacency. It couldn't have happened at a better time.

Women's Lib demonstration

6

Tides of Change

At times the elements combine to produce unusual physical phenomena such as the king tide: a rise of tide about twice as high as normal. It happens only when a strong inshore wind blows during those hours, about once a fortnight, when the rise of the tide will be naturally higher than usual.

So in the affairs of man a rare combination of factors can occur to produce an unanticipated result. The late 1960s and early 1970s saw such a king tide in Australia: the sudden recognition that we have many specifically Australian things which merit our pride and care. This has led to the beginnings of effective Australian identity—a feeling of pride in and being at home with and attuned to the Australian environment and community.

It is quite difficult to determine why, at a time when more newcomers were pouring into Australia than at any period since the gold rush, there should have been this definite upsurge of interest in everything Australian. Perhaps it was the knowledge that Mother England was deliberately shedding the load of her Empire and leaving it to forge its own future. Perhaps a turning away from the 'all the way with LBJ' attitude of the early 1960s. Or maybe it was a simple expression of maturity: of a nation growing up and beginning to feel that it could rely upon itself

Modern housing estate at Elizabeth, SA

instead of others.

There have been many outward demonstrations of this feeling. The commonest is the sudden passionate dedication to Australian native plants. Writers of a century ago such as Anthony Trollope and Marcus Clarke bemoaned the monotony of Australian flora and it seems that most people agreed with them, because they dug, slashed, and burned until they created a wilderness which they then replanted with exotics. Often these needed excessive care—and excessive water—to stay alive in Australia.

All at once, groups of gardening enthusiasts joined in more and more associations for the promotion of Australian native plants. The Australian wildflower garden in Canberra showed what could be done, and similar gardens were established in other cities. The enthusiasts promoted, cajoled, propagandised, and had working bees to plant roadsides with native plants. The landscape gardeners of developers and government authorities joined in the fashion, and as new suburbs and towns grew up so did the stands of native plants. Elizabeth, the new town established north of Adelaide in the 1950s, now has flourishing groves and copses of many varieties of eucalypt.

Finally the home gardeners joined in, and appreciation of the subtle beauty, fast-growing strength, and delicate fragrance of

Australian wildflower garden, Canberra

himself, and those who chose to join him, a genuinely Australian mode of life. After much searching he found some 200 acres of natural bushland near Hurstbridge in Victoria, where he built a timber and adobe-brick house and studio, using bricks made by himself and a group of friends. He regarded his house as something which would continue to grow and change. As he said to me, 'You shouldn't really build a house from some artificial and imposed plan. You find a great old door, a piece of ironwork, some beaut stone, and start to build around it.'

Cliff's house, Dunmoochin, nestles on a wooded ridge and is surrounded by a fenced area in which there are kangaroos, wallabies and emus. The house is ruled by a pet wombat and a sulphur-crested cockatoo and, of course, Cliff's wife, Judith.

A community of artists concerned with the Australian scene grew up around

Clifton Pugh in his studio

Australian natives is now more firmly established than ever before. Edna Everage would now be more likely to grow grevillea than gladioli.

The community was also influenced by an artistic élite. After the war, a number of artists and craftsmen was concerned by the materialism, alienation, and crass ugliness of suburbia. They resolved to create craft-based integrated communities which were more attuned to natural surroundings. Such a community grew up at Warrandyte in Victoria and aroused so much interest and curiosity that it was besieged by Sunday drivers. Another was inspired by Clifton Pugh, the superb landscape artist who is also one of Australia's most successful portrait painters. He was determined to create for

Dunmoochin. Two outstanding potters, Leon and Ruth Saper, live in a house devised by Morrie Shaw that is quite fascinating. The land was not levelled, and the bricks were laid over the natural line of the ground, so that the floor is free-flowing and undulating. Rough-hewn pillars of wood, with some door

Gate in Clifton Pugh's garden

and window frames, support chicken-wire onto which Shaw plastered waterproofed adobe to form a free flowing igloo-like roof and walls. Additional light comes through beer bottle bottoms set in the walls. Inside there are no separate rooms, but adobe partitions to divide activity.

It is a house at one with its surroundings: cosy, welcoming, and beautiful. As elsewhere in Dunmoochin, there is no attempt at formal gardening. The garden consists of the natural surroundings, immeasurably older than the human habitations, which have been adapted to them instead of vice versa.

But it was not merely in lifestyle that Cliff Pugh and his friends affected Australians' view of themselves. Cliff and his neighbour Albert Tucker, together with Russell Drysdale, Sydney Nolan, Fred Williams and Frank Hodgkinson, presented the Australian scene to Australians in all its vivid harshness

Open-air market, St Andrews, Vic

and intensity, quite differently from Heysen's mellow gentleness. Another artist who has succeeded in 'popularising' the Australian landscape more than any predecessor is Pro Hart, and it is significant that his idiosyncratic paintings in almost savage colours, peopled by stark and forlorn figures, have not met with the approval of art critics.

Australians, influenced often unwittingly by the perception of the artists, began to identify with and no longer feel alienated from their own country. New developers no longer felt the need to create English-like suburbs. Stands of gums were retained and featured. And architecture has in some significant areas improved to accord with local conditions. At long last one may see homes planned and built to harmonise with their environment although they still tend to be in the minority. The kitsch of speculative developers, who build Cape Cod homes with roof lines pitched

The Sapers' house, Dunmoochin, Vic

to shed North American snow, and fake Colonial and fake Spanish and fake 'contemporary', is still distressingly prevalent.

The results of all this new-felt identification with our own environment coincided with

59

Ayers House, Adelaide, is a fine example of an historic building once neglected but now restored to its original appearance. It now houses National Trust headquarters and two restaurants

concern, quickly communicated to Australia from America, at the environmental damage caused by DDT and other pesticides. The groundswell of demand for care of the environment grew greater here than elsewhere in the world—because it met and filled a long-felt need. Australians became enthusiastic conservationists, not only because they were convinced intellectually of the need for greater care for themselves and their children's future, but because the realisation of the need to care for the environment caused them at last to identify with it.

In the 1950s and 1960s, pleas on my part to preserve and not to destroy community assets brought little community response or public

an emotional need for Australians. Until the 1970s Australian history meant little in physical terms to most Australians. Oh yes, there had been the Rum Rebellion, Macquarie, the Gold Rush and the Eureka Stockade, Billy Hughes and Conscription, Gallipoli and the Kokoda Trail, but no sermons in stones or books in running brooks. What was not recent was regarded not so much as historic, as old hat and outmoded. Old buildings were not restored, they were 'modernised'. But, quite suddenly, people began to realise that history—a rootedness in society—is evidenced around us by what our forebears built.

In the early 1960s my outcries over the planned destruction of Adelaide's historic Theatre Royal—a beautiful, charming and elegant baroque theatre which had provided much of the State's important theatrical occasion—aroused no murmur from the public generally. I was condemned for holding up 'progress' and the antique building redolent of the past was wrecked and a car park built in its place. But in 1970 I had no trouble at all when I devoted a large sum of public money to acquiring an old bank building simply to preserve it for posterity. There was nothing original about it—it was a piece of 'Chamber of Commerce Baroque'— utterly derivative of an earlier period of European architecture, yet in its genre a piece of great workmanship. Now called Edmund Wright House, it is a place of pride for many South Australians.

A sense of identity with landscape, with town, and with history is essential to the development of the creative and integrated human personality. The king tide of change in the early 1970s made possible the emergence of a real sense of Australian identity in the suburbs of Australian cities.

How is it developing—and what is its future?

support in South Australia. But by 1970 a high school student became quite violent during one of my election speeches, because I failed to mention the environment!

But conservation is not merely concerned with our natural surroundings. It also involves preservation of the good things in the man-made environment, and that again fulfils

7

Zuzza Bwogga Leads the Way

Happily, the rising feeling of Australian identity coincided with the arrival in Australia of a mood and attitude to suburban existence which had affected American urban renewal for a decade.

People woke up to the fact that by moving out to the sprawling, low density suburbs they were depriving themselves of many of the advantages of urban existence, most of which are best obtained by proximity to central urban facilities. In America, the affluent started to buy up old houses in the centre of cities—the genuine 'town houses' built in rows or terraces. They restored them and lived in them and gained all the advantages of central city life, combined often enough with the ability to make a retreat to a country hideout.

In Australia, people were still reluctant to move back to live in the central business district. Zoning laws had for so long said, 'Industry here, commerce there, residence somewhere else.' The idea of mixed function areas, like those of European cities, was hard to revive in a country which for generations had put up buildings for each separate function of existence.

But the immediate suburbs, just beyond the city business district, became attractive. Paddington, in Sydney, was the first to bloom. Purchase and restoration of terrace

Terrace homes at Paddington, Sydney

houses, many of them almost derelict after the decades of lemming-like movement to the suburbs, and the refurbishing of 'Paddington lace', became the rage. With it came a pride in the history of the old suburb; residents' associations; good eateries; a sense of neighbourhood. The movement spread. In Melbourne, such areas as Fitzroy and Carlton, North Melbourne, Richmond and St Kilda experienced similar restoration.

In Adelaide, which had only a few row houses, the refurbishing took place in the bluestone cottages of Norwood, Kensington, St Peters, Walkerville, North Adelaide, and Lower North Adelaide. The last two not only produced historians and a residents' association, but a street market and an active

Renovated bluestone home, St Peters, SA

community pub life. A lively sense of the importance of neighbourhood developed.

The restorations, important aesthetically and to preserve a sense of history, were for the most part carried out sensibly and creatively. People understood the mistakes of the original builders in not adapting their concepts to the environment. They stripped away ugly lean-to laundries, kitchens, and bathrooms from the rear of buildings, and created private gardens and courtyards which could give pleasant living conditions.

An interest in and concern for the history of local areas excited the new residents and interested the old. The case of Kent Town, in South Australia, may be cited as an example. Kent Town is a suburb on the edge of the central city district. Its population has fallen by two-thirds in the last twenty years and it has suffered a rash of light industries and the ugly redevelopment of old homes into commercial buildings. It is certainly not the most attractive part of the old Adelaide area. But when the historian of the Kensington and Norwood municipality, the suburb next door, announced a 'walk through old Kent Town', 300 people joined him as he walked the streets and pointed out the historical development of the suburb during 120 years. In Sydney, the demand for the preservation of the Rocks area and old Woolloomooloo roused people to passion and demonstration.

There was some danger to the poor and underprivileged in all this. As inner city areas became more fashionable, the poor who had previously inhabited them, with the advantage

Graffiti on old homes at Woolloomooloo give two sides of a story

of low rentals and small transport costs, were evicted and priced out of the market. They were pushed from poor housing in the centre of the city to often even poorer housing at the periphery, with greater isolation and with transport costs they could ill afford.

In the USA 'urban renewal' had often gone hand in hand with 'poor removal'. In South Australia we were determined that the poor and the less fortunate would participate in inner suburban rejuvenation. The S.A. Housing Trust consequently bought many of the old cottages, refurbished them and let them at concessional rentals to previous tenants. Where rebuilding had to take place because dilapidation had gone too far, medium density complexes to fit in with the surroundings were provided for needy families. In one suburb an old factory was made over as a community centre.

In the inner suburb of Hackney the whole local community was engaged with the Housing Trust in planning effective local redevelopment—retaining what could be

Creche at Richmond, Melbourne

refurbished, rebuilding for needy families and students.

As this ferment bubbled in the old inner suburbs, the need for local community involvement infected numbers of outer suburbs. In many parts of the outer suburban wilderness, community feeling woke to life and demanded community facilities and local involvement.

Citizens in these areas began to ask for community welfare centres, playgrounds and creches, community medical centres, and eventually the planning of regional urban nodes to establish central city facilities in the outer suburbs. People looked critically at their streetscapes, perhaps for the first time, and demanded an end to the 'Great Australian Ugliness'.

The realisation that traditional Australian housing is ill-adapted to our climate and our preferred Australian way of life has been slow to dawn. But it has affected the way in which old houses have been restored, and it has enabled some really discernible improvements in architecture.

This had long been a hobby-horse of mine. South Australia, like the rest of Australia south of a line from, say, Brisbane in the east to Geraldton in the west, has a Mediterranean climate where one may take advantage of living outdoors. There is limited need to huddle indoors for most of the year, and I believed that the best way to live was to have a house on the northern side of a street, built close to the street across the southern frontage. The living areas of the house could thus be glass-walled to the north, opening into a completely private garden area, with pergolas on which grape-vines were trained to give summer shade and winter sun. And that's how I built my own home. I wake up in the mornings to birdsong in my trees and feel 'I like living here!' The garden has no lawn, and no plants which require heavy watering. It

Don Dunstan in his garden

has shrubs, trees, tan-bark and ground cover with trickle watering—a great Australian invention. It can be kept in order with a minimum of effort and it is peaceful, restful and attractive.

I can walk into the garden from the large living area, which contains facilities for cooking, dining, playing music, and sitting about, or from my bedroom. The area shaded by the pergola is an extension of the living area of the house, and much used for this purpose. Close handy is the outdoor barbecue and swimming pool—all the facilities to take advantage of one of the most equable climates in the world with more hours of fine sunshine than any comparable city anywhere.

More and more Australians are coming to terms with their urban environment with similar enthusiasm. We have a long road to travel before we leave behind the atrocious taste and sheer inconvenience peddled by some spec builders. But we are on the way.

In city centres, in outer suburbs, and in new developments, the realisation is dawning that the new drive to make our suburban areas into communities and social activity centres, instead of geographic collections of isolated individuals, requires better opportunities for unhurried pedestrian intermingling. Malls are being provided in city centres, with varying degrees of success depending upon the adequacy of their planning. Also many suburbs now understand that they need to replan the mode of movement of residents so that their areas are more pedestrian-oriented. The local community as well as the private house must become a home instead of a dormitory.

In Glebe, in Sydney, the Federal Labor Government purchased the ancient property of the Church of England. The suburb was decayed, physically and socially. The houses were run down, the area was slashed through by freeways, and the isolation and alienation

The Mall in Launceston, Tasmania, is one example of the reinvigoration of Australian city centres

68

of the people were evident in rising juvenile crime, alcoholism and drug addiction.

But, given an opportunity, the community set to with a will. In 1974, a group of residents formed the 'Woolley Centre'. Morrie Shaw, lecturer in architecture, whom we previously met as creator of the Saper house, was appointed director. The Centre acts as a resource centre for the Glebe development plan. As part of this plan, it encourages and guides community involvement, and channels the energies of local residents into activities for children and young people. At last, the Centre has shown that planning could and should get away from the experts and the drawing-boards and out among the people— the people for whom such planning is often done in theory but with little genuine recognition of their emotional needs.

The Centre started after-school and vacation workshops, and then, with the help of a team of architecture students, undertook some exciting school playground projects which inspired enormous excitement, interest and social activity.

With the maximum participation of children, parents, and other citizens the 'Zuzza Bwogga' was built in the Glebe school playground. It is a pinewood playhouse which is quite complex and gives opportunity for play of a kind *which the children want*. (In Norwood we have an 'adventure playground' erected by the Education Department into which I rarely see a child venture!)

The Zuzza Bwogga incorporates a small intimate open-air theatre with performance areas at several levels. Free-form seating was built and then decorated with tiles. Over a period 'Tile-ins' were held, with kids and adults all doing a bit of design and tiling— expressing themselves in a piece of community decoration. Fairs and street markets were held in conjunction with the tile-ins. The new sense of excitement and community involvement is rapidly making Glebe a community where people live with

69

The Zuzza Bwogga

pleasure and pride.

A similar revitalisation is evident in other parts of other cities. Many new suburbs are being planned on the Radburn principle, which keeps cars on the periphery of the area and does not permit car-occupied roadways between houses, schools and community centres, and service shops.

At West Lakes, in South Australia, the Housing Trust has provided an excellent example of this type of planning, in marked contrast to the traditional-style earlier development at Elizabeth.

The larger Australian country towns never suffered the problems of suburban alienation. They had always had some sense of community, a greater degree of effective social intercourse, a better sense of identity with place. But as the sense of Australian identity and community grew in the suburbs of the cities, the same mood led to heightened community activity in the country. This mood and activity were evidenced in Cairns, in Wagga, in Bendigo and Ballarat, in Mount Gambier and the River Murray towns, in Geraldton and Launceston.

It was paralleled by an exodus of city dwellers to live the good life in the country, even though they may still have to earn wages in the city. Despite the problems of commuting, the most dramatic evidence of this trend has occurred in New South Wales. There has been a steady exodus from Sydney. The 1976 census showed a 26,000 decrease in Sydney's population accompanied by an increase of residents in the shires along the coast north and south of the city. The great Australian dream for many people is a return to the soil. They do not want to live as full-time farmers, but as part-time or hobby farmers. Australia has always been a nation of house-owners, and now many people have extended the home-owning motive into the ownership of a larger plot of land and the pleasures of a rural life, supplemented by a non-rural income. Many Australians reject the materialism of our mass-consumption society, They want to grow their own food, produce some for sale, and have a place for themselves and their children to roam, play, and keep a horse.

Surveys in Lismore in New South Wales, and Lilydale and Kilmore in Victoria, show a high proportion of part-time farmers. Only a tiny proportion receive the largest proportion of their income from the land. Some were originally full-time farmers, forced to take work in the towns or cities when their incomes from farm production fell away, and some, of course, are city people trying to use farms for tax losses. But those people are less and less a feature of the rural scene. The overwhelming majority are people whose main income has always been from other sources. They simply wanted to live in a rural environment instead of the 'red brick jungle' of the suburbs.

The hobby-farmers are usually good about caring for the land. There have been complaints that they allow their land to deteriorate, do not clear weeds, and endanger nearby properties through their neglect. But government investigation in three States has shown that the majority of hobby farmers are careful husbandmen. Often the land has not deteriorated at all. In most cases they improved its beauty and its productive capacity, because they work for the love of it.

Conflicts rapidly arose. Those who were first to go to the near countryside, to live on a hobby farm and commute to the city or country centre, naturally wanted to prevent others from doing so. They expected taxpayers generally to compensate local

landowners, in order to prevent development which would change the previously rural character of such areas.

But, on the whole, the impetus has been to take a pride and delight in local history; to improve, but in a way which preserves and

Steven Wright's home

restores rather than changes and destroys; to identify with Australian qualities of the landscape; to take part in the local community.

This type of development has been typified by my Private Secretary, Steven Wright, and his wife Margit. Five years ago they bought an original Australian farmhouse: the first built in the area of Inglewood and Paracombe in the Adelaide Hills, seventeen miles from the city. With it went five acres of land, mostly planted to Doradilla grapes, and some old stables. The house had been built in three stages. The first, built in about 1840, was the typical settlers' 'backender' of one room and a kitchen, made of limestone quarried from the site and plastered together with pug. Two more rooms were added some years later, and a two-roomed pitched roof cottage built

Street scene, Bendigo

around the turn of the century. All the woodwork was worm-eaten, the roof leaked, and the kitchen and bathroom still had an earthen floor simply overlaid with several layers of lino. On the outside of the house, various lean-to's of corrugated iron and fibre—board were uncomfortable later excrescences.

Steven and Margit have worked for years to make this into one of the most delightful spots in the Adelaide Hills. They slated the cottage roof, slated the kitchen floor, rebuilt the bathroom, and replaced the woodwork. They knocked down the excrescences, made a wide patio, and built on an extension, with wide verandahs, in keeping with the older part of the house. They landscaped the old garden with terraces edged with dry stone walling, of stone which Steven carried from a ruined house nearby and built into the terraces under the tuition of his Cornish

grandfather, and retained the old exotics grown by the first settlers but also planted over a thousand native trees and shrubs (some of them with my help).

But in all this they didn't just spend their time making a nest for themselves. They have joined the local community—the orchardists of the area—and taken active part in both the organised and informal social life of their own area. They have a real and satisfying identity with the past and present of their district.

This pug and timber barn at Paechtown in the Mount Lofty Ranges shows how settlers began to use local materials

8

'Whingeing Poms' and Others

No book on the changing mood of modern Australia would be complete without an account of the profound effect that post-war migration has had upon this country. Next to Israel, Australia since 1945 has had the biggest proportionate increase in population through migration of any country in the world.

During the years of high migration intake Australia maintained (I believe quite improperly) the 'white Australia' policy. Consequently the migrants were overwhelmingly Caucasian. The first wave was of refugees, largely Lithuanian, Latvian and Estonian, plus Ukrainians and other nationalities, who had been freed from the German work camps. They contained a higher proportion of middle-class and professional people than existed in the general Australian population at that time, but the assistance given to them in migrant camps and hostels to assimilate into the general community was minimal. However, they were already used to the privations of refugee status in wartime. They turned to with a will and took every opportunity to create a settled existence of reasonable affluence in Australia, and motivated their children to higher education. Very soon after their arrival they set up community centres and clubs of their own to help each other and to cherish the

Faces of Australia: Sikhs at Woolgoolga, NSW

folk ways and customs of their homeland. Now, about thirty years later, the results are well apparent. The migrants from those countries have thoroughly integrated into the Australian community and many have become substantial businessmen or have made successful 'second lives' for themselves in other ways, but at the same time they have added a little of the flavour of their homelands to the changing Australian scene. And, equally important, all their sons and daughters have grown up to regard themselves as wholly Australian and have become a vital part of our community, especially because their parents laid such emphasis upon the need for education and trade skills.

The first wave of migration was followed by a steady torrent of assisted migration from various parts of Europe and later, from many parts of the world. Some, like the South Africans and Rhodesians and Chileans who have come to Australia during the past few years, sought freedom from oppressive regimes in their homelands. The overwhelming majority came in search of a life better than they might expect if they stayed at home. Encouraged by Australian immigration authorities, and in a good many cases by cheap fares or heavy subsidies towards their passage money, they poured into Australia from Britain, Italy, Greece, and Jugoslavia. Political upheavals such as the

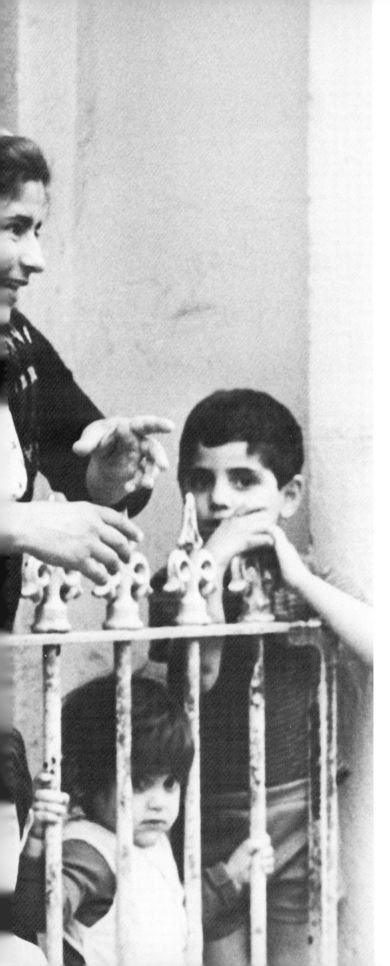

Suez crisis and Hungarian rebellion of 1956 brought fresh communities of refugees. The independence of India from the British Raj prompted a good many Eurasians to seek a more secure community. The independence of Indonesia, the traditional recipient of migratory Hollanders, caused a steady flow from Holland into Australia. As the years went by, the Australian ethnic mix was added to by Germans, Scandinavians, Turks, Bulgarians, and Spaniards.

The largest migrant communities consist of British, Italians, and Greeks. (It is said that Melbourne is the third largest Greek city in the world!). There have been marked differences in the settlement modes of these three communities, although they all came from peoples who have traditionally migrated from small and crowded homelands to seek fortune overseas.

In the 1940s and early 1950s the British came to Australia from a country drab with the aftermath of a fearsome war. In Britain, all necessities were strictly rationed until the mid-1950s, luxuries were non-existent, overseas travel almost impossible, and everyday life restricted by a maze of regulations. Nevertheless the migrants were convinced that the welfare state envisaged in the Beveridge Report published in 1943, and offered as one of the rewards of winning the war, was a viable proposal. Hence the overwhelming Labour victory in the 1945 elections.

Proud of their part in the defeat of Hitler and expectant of even greater freedom and opportunity in Australia, the British came here in shiploads from 1946 onwards. Many were fast disillusioned. First they encountered the dual personality of old-style Australians, who expressed admiration for British achievements but treated individual 'Pommies' as inferiors. They found that Australia, which had encouraged them to emigrate, could not

Faces of Australia: Paddington family

77

Faces of Australia: Henryk Lewicki from Poland

even provide housing for her own people. The migrants were lodged in hostels, usually consisting of army huts. The conditions in these 'migrant camps' were accepted patiently at first, but as the years passed with no sign of improvement, and any protests treated as 'Pommy whingeing', they broke into open rebellion.

In 1952 the Menzies government promulgated new boarding charges in the hostels. Effectively, these left each migrant family with £2 per week to cover all their living expenses apart from board and lodging, and to save up to get out of the hostel!

The migrants challenged the government in the courts, and in South Australia I acted as their counsel.

The High Court declared the charges illegal, which gave the British migrants some immediate relief but left many with a sense of resentment against Australian government.

South Australia accepted more than its proportion of British migrants, and the State government worked as fast as possible to provide them with homes, at a time when there was a severe housing shortage throughout Australia and the banks and the Federal government were very tight with housing finance. The South Australian Housing Trust bought a number of prefabricated houses and rapidly created new suburbs, while continuing with bricks and mortar construction in others and planning the new town of Elizabeth.

However life in the new suburbs was not particularly easy. Usually there was only one income, because employment for wives was

harder to find in those days, and a man had to pay his mortgage, buy furniture and other household goods, and buy some kind of motor transport because the new suburbs were far from commercial and industrial areas and public transport was poor. In other States the picture was similar. The same conditions applied to many 'Old Australians', of course, but at least they were at home in their own country with the support of relations and friends. They could not appreciate the migrants' problems of isolation and adjustment, especially for the wives and

Australian profile: Drinker in Brisbane hotel

children, in Australian suburbia where there was no settled communal life, no local loyalty, no single thing to support a feeling of identity and home—not even a friendly local pub of the type in which British people were accustomed to relax in the evenings. But the

Faces of Australia: an elderly Italian migrant dons his old Carabinieri uniform

78

wise migrant soon learnt to keep his mouth shut. If he criticised such conditions, in the way that countless Australians criticise them nowadays, he was promptly labelled a 'whingeing Pom'.

It took about twenty years for the new communities to develop a sense of life as genuine communities. Sporting and social clubs grew, pub life more like that of England prospered. And the timing of the lessening of the difficulties of British migrant communities—the disappearance of the feeling that they were in some sort of British 'ghetto' —coincided with the tidal feeling in city suburbs which I have earlier described.

The Italian and Greek settlers, from countries without the welfare state background of the British, displayed quite different behaviour and expectations.

Street stand to advise migrants on naturalisation formalities

Faces of Australia: Italian lady, Flemington, NSW

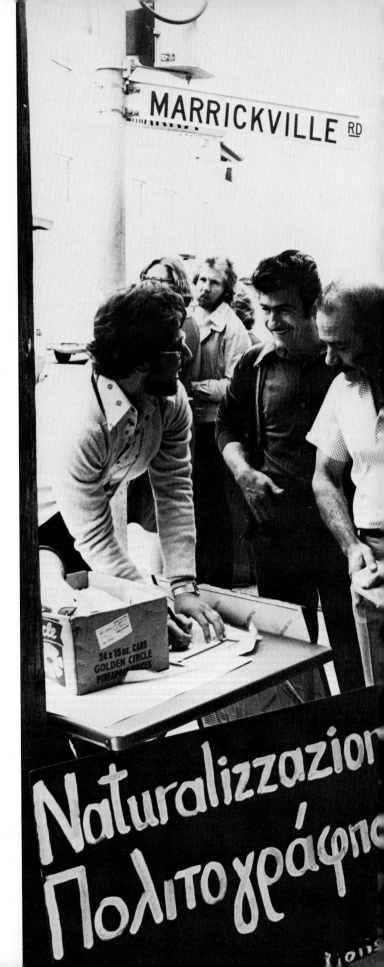

80

Regional and family association in migration were, among them, quite marked. Coming, for the most part, from conditions less affluent and more crowded than those of the average Australian with whom they worked, they saw diligence and thrift as a means to rapid betterment of their situation. In many cases their first move was to buy a ramshackle old house available cheaply in an inner suburb, and work hard to improve it. This was possible before the inner suburbs came back into fashion and prices began to soar. Often, such a home would provide a base for two or three families and some single men from the home town or province. From this base they could, by family and group financing, enable numbers of their people to move out and build in newer suburbs. Many Italians entered the building industry, and built houses for themselves and a few flats to let.

But both the Greek and Italian

Faces of Australia: Greek grandfather, Melbourne

Paddy's Market, Ultimo, NSW

communities were socially deprived and
isolated. In earlier years, the average
Australian was even more chauvinistically
inclined towards these migrants than he was
towards the British, and many of the migrants
found it was very difficult to learn English
and communicate with their fellow workers
or gain knowledge and information from the
media. Consequently the Italians banded
together in regional clubs, such as the
Venezia, Fogolar Furlan, Azzuri, Napoli. In

Faces of Australia: Italian bambino

Sydney the Apia Club, and the Italian Club at
Fairfield, mirrored for Italians the Leagues
Clubs of the Aussies.

The Greeks were bound together more than
the Italians by two influences. In Greece, the
church is traditionally a secular community
centre as well as a place of worship, and
Greek social and family custom is even more
markedly different from the Anglo-Saxon
norm in Australia than is the Italian. The

Service in the Greek Orthodox Archdiocese of Australia,
Melbourne

Faces of Australia: the watermelon man, Flemington Market

Greeks have formed some associations based on homeland affiliations, such as the Macedonians and the Cypriots, but these have not had the importance or cohesive influence of the Orthodox Church. Unfortunately there has been a schism within this church in Australia, and this has created real tensions in the Greek community.

Many second-generation Greeks have not assimilated into Australian society as readily as most of their Italian counterparts. They have worked as hard as the Italians and in many cases have prospered, but they have steadily accumulated a justified resentment that Australian society has ignored the very real social deprivations to which they have been subjected. These deprivations arise from a kind of vicious circle: language problems and social differences which make it difficult for Greeks and Australians to understand each other, so that the Australians make only token attempts to do so and the Greek community becomes even more introverted

and less responsive to outsiders. However the situation has not been helped by some remarkably clumsy governmental actions such as the closing of the Melbourne ethnic radio station 3JJ.

The Yugoslavs have adapted in different ways according to the States in which they settled. In Western Australia, where a large (mainly Croatian) community had existed before the war and was loyal to the Allied cause during the war, the post-war migration did not cause splits in the Yugoslav community. But in some other States the migrants have imported the hatreds and bitterness of race, language and historic divisions in Yugoslavia. There is a substantial Yugoslav community in South Australia, but whenever I refer to it publicly I receive indignant letters from Croats and Macedonians claiming that there is no such people!

By and large, however, the Yugoslavs have integrated well, as have Poles, Spaniards, Czechs, Hungarians and Dutch—whose migrant communities are smaller than those I have so far dealt with.

Faces of Australia: Farmer, northern NSW

84

Saturday morning outside the Yugoslav Ethnic School, Newtown, NSW

The German migration has been of particular significance to South Australia, given the fact that from the first settlement of the State it had had a considerable German component. Germans in South Australia could find a settled, wealthy and influential German element already here. The result is that the Germans in South Australia have been outstanding in their public effect upon Australian life style.

German food, social jollity and *gemütlichkeit* are evident in the Barossa Valley with its now enormous tourist trade and its biennial vintage festival, in villages like Hahndorf (traditionally the centre of German culture in South Australia) and in the annual Schuetzenfest. German clubs are active centres of jollity in all major centres in Australia, and Goethe Societies exist to preserve interest in the German language and literature.

There is a good deal of social ferment among migrants in Australia who feel that 'Old Australians' have neglected them and their problems: imported them into the country and then left them to sink or swim.

Of course this is a traditional problem. The very first generation of white people born in Australia jeered at the 'Jimmy Raws' arriving from England early last century. British and Australian miners assaulted Chinese migrants who arrived during the gold rush. Chauvinistic contempt for non-Australians was firmly established by the turn of the century, but after all the Australians have been no guiltier in this respect than the

Street festival. Lithuanian dancers, Clifton Hill, Vic

Faces of Australia: pupil at Glebe Primary School, NSW

eager to contribute from it to the social life of Australia. It stood in dire need of these migrant contributions. The isolation of suburban existence needed to be countered by the emergence of the new social impulses which I have already described, and the communal life of cities and suburbs needed the togetherness, the fun, the revelry, the joy of good food and good companionship so much more evident in the social life of

Faces of Australia: children in Flemington Market

Americans, themselves originally British, who despised and then assimilated the English, Irish, Italians, Scandinavians, Ashkenazi Jews, Poles, Germans, and many other races during successive waves of migration. The only difference is that we say 'Pommies' and the Americans say 'Limeys'.

And one must admit that the easiest way to deal with a problem is to ignore it, in the hope that it will go away. We ignored the problems of the Aborigines, and many other Australian social problems, for a good many years until various dedicated folk obliged us to look at them squarely. The same has applied to migrant problems. Only of recent years have we abandoned the attitude of 'Nobody forced 'em to come here. Now that they're here let them make the best of it'.

Nevertheless the migrant communities, with pride in their own heritage, have been

European cities, towns, and villages. The life of the Italian trattoria, English pub, German beer garden, Hungarian cafe, and the Greek square were all missing. The migrants have had their greatest influence in demonstrating to Australians as a whole that the company of their fellows is good.

The famed Australian 'mateship' was a fellow-feeling for immediate, known, and proven friends. Beyond it Australians had an intuitive reserve and an Anglo-Saxon apprehension about anything unfamiliar: an apprehension which often found expression in chauvinism.

The most easily-perceived migrant influence has taken place in Australian food. Italians and Hungarians to the greatest extent, but all migrant groups in their own way, have influenced Australian food habits for the better. No longer is the dripping pot a feature of every Australian housewife's kitchen.

But it is in public occasions of jollity that they have been a catalyst for what is now a marked feature of Australian life. The

Above: Faces of Australia: Caterina Cavuoto and her daughter Elisa Betta   Hectorville, SA   *Below:* In the Cafe Sport, Leichhardt, Sydney

migrants have emerged from their clubs, where they have been nurturing their native song and dance and training their young in the folk ways of homeland, to teach

settlements all over the country they are happening. Jacaranda Festivals, Orange Festivals, Almond Blossom Festivals, Wine Bushing Festivals, Poinsettia Festivals—and they are all fun. They are part of the evident emergence of a confidence and pride in Australian society, in its place as home.

Faces of Australia: Christophe, a French boy

Australians generally that there is an Italian, a Greek, a German, a Yugoslav, a Polish, a Latvian, Lithuanian, Estonian, Ukrainian tradition which is also Australian, and as Australian as the Anglo-Saxon heritage. And it has brought those of British descent out to display their folkways and traditions, too. When I proposed the establishment of a Cornish Festival, in Australia's 'Little Cornwall', people of Cornish descent came flocking. The staid citizens of the three towns were soon dancing the Furry Dance in the streets of Wallaroo.

Festivaliana has bloomed in Australia. From the Adelaide Festival of Arts, Melbourne's Moomba, Perth's Art Festival, Sydney's Festival to little towns and

Inner suburban children, Darlington, Sydney

9

We're All Going Back to School

One of the most significant festivals is one of the least formal—a festival of, for and organised by children in Adelaide—the 'Come Out'.

And, speaking of children, that leads us to education. Until the fairly recent past, school life and home life in Australia were strictly segregated. When students left school they rarely returned. Apart from homework, the life of the school was not seen as being involved with home at all. Other than for those who undertook some form of tertiary education, a comparative few until about twenty years ago, general learning was thought to come to an end with the end of school attendance. Adult education was undertaken by only a small minority, through University extension classes or such organisations as the Workers' Education Association. Even then, the primary and secondary school buildings were rarely used for such purposes. After school hours they were dark.

Educators and community leaders could pontificate on the theme that education was part of life and should continue throughout one's life, but it made little dent in the wall of public indifference.

But the 1970s brought a revolution in education, in the use of schools and their place in the community. Until this decade,

Making gingerbread men in a modern pre-school

Australia had underspent every comparable country on education. England, the USA, Canada, New Zealand, France, Italy, West Germany, the Scandinavian countries, Belgium and the Netherlands all spent more per capita on education than Australia. It is true we were doing better than Greece, Iceland and Turkey, but that was small comfort.

When the Labor Government came to power in Canberra in 1972, their platform ensured that national resources would be so reorganised that education would receive a massive infusion of funds, a task which they accomplished.

It was done at a time when use could be made of the money to allow experiment in new forms of education which not only changed its mode but also affected its relationship to the home.

Open classroom: Kilkenny, SA

The degree of experiment varies from State to State, and the greatest change occurred in South Australia. Perhaps it was most needed here. I well remember when, as a new young member of Parliament, I visited the local infant school. It was a demonstration school for student teachers, ruled by a principal who was a martinet (or should it be martinette?). She took me to see some area of the playground where the asphalt had broken up, and spotted a small boy engaged in some minor transgression. 'Come here, that boy,' she rasped. She beckoned him to her, clutched his small hand, and dragged the terrified child round the school while she listed her complaints to me. Finally she let the child go with severe admonitions, and then told me she had forgotten she still had him 'in tow'.

Today the picture is entirely different. At that same school I am likely to be met not by a teacher but by a small child who takes me by the hand and says, 'Come and see what I'm doing.' In each room an informal teaching method is used with each child being separately programmed. Of course, much of the teaching is in groups, but the groups are flexible according to particular needs.

The conditions of home life are more nearly mirrored by school, and although work is organised, it is nevertheless possible for each child to participate creatively rather than passively. I know there is much criticism from traditionalists of the open space flexible group method of teaching, but I have vivid memories that under the 'chalk and talk' imposed discipline method, twenty-seven per cent of children leaving primary school were in need of remedial teaching. The drop-out rate in early years of tertiary education caused constant wails, but stemmed from the fact that many students found it difficult to make the considerable jump from the imposed discipline of school teaching to the self-discipline and increased motivation for study required by the lecture and tutorial method of tertiary institutions.

Today, in some parts of Australia and certainly in South Australia, we are setting out to encourage self-motivation and participation as the basis not only of learning but of life. Instead of requiring each child to conform to the 'norm', i.e. the level and pace of teaching which is too fast for the dull and too slow for the bright, education is now geared to cope with each child's weaknesses and disabilities. His or her strengths are encouraged and developed at the most suitable pace.

Because the new initiatives are undertaken by the children themselves, and because the atmosphere of the school no longer seems so alienated from that of home, the schools are rapidly becoming more involved with the life of the community, the neighbourhood and the home. And no longer are the schools dark after normal school hours. The buildings and classrooms are used by adults of every age from eighteen to eighty, taking advantage of the enormous new programmes of Adult Education and Further Education which cover a staggering variety of subjects. At long last, education really is continuous throughout life.

We have a long way to go to the ideal, but the hopeful signs are there. In Grenoble, in France, I went to see a workers' housing centre. It was high rise, high density, and in fact a prime example of what we should not do in Australia. But there were features of the whole development which had a great lesson for us. The school was a family education, information, resource and recreation centre. It was in constant use during the whole of waking hours. It was connected on closed-circuit TV to all the units in the development. Much of what was presented in the school thus went straight to the living rooms of all residents. All community groups used it to publicise their activities. It was a centre for community life and learning in a very real sense.

We are still far short of this stage—but we are moving. In the S.A. Housing Trust's village at West Lakes, the whole pedestrian precinct has been built round the school as a community centre, which it effectively is.

One of the suburban wastelands of the Adelaide metropolis, the area comprising Mansfield Park, Angle Park, and their neighbouring suburbs, was a region of comparatively low-income families, few public facilities, and poor community services. With the enthusiastic support of local residents, a plan was developed to transform the school into the Parks Community Centre, and to make it a place of constant use and enjoyment for a wide range of community activity. With finance from the Federal Labor Government, the project proceeded as a pilot project of its type for Australia. So far it has been resoundingly successful. It has generated an entirely new feeling and heart in that area of suburbia.

In Burra, an old copper-mining and rural centre, proposals for a new high school were modified by community-generated demands for a community college. Instead of dealing only with students up to matriculation level, it was to include schooling at all levels, and provide an effective centre for community cultural and educational activity. The proposal was accepted and a $3 million complex is currently being built as a prototype for similar developments in other country areas.

The school at Loxton, on the Murray River, received a grant for a hall. The local community promptly banded together to make it a community hall, and the result is a splendid little theatre which is a centre for the town's cultural activities, not just for school plays and assemblies.

This movement will strengthen, together with other great revolutions in education which have taken place so swiftly and effectively that the average person is not aware of them.

Adult and Further Education have had an enormous boom. The days of a few people

Don Dunstan's wife, Adele Koh, gives lessons in Chinese cooking

attending WEA or University extension courses for after-hours technical training have gone. The biggest expansion in education activities has been in the further education field. In some areas of Australia, and particularly in South Australia, the evening enrolment of adults in classes at schools exceeds the daytime enrolment of pupils of school age.

Courses have been established, according to demand, over an enormously wide range, from technical training in mechanics and electronics to literature and the humanities and crafts.

In South Australia, eleven courses were undertaken in Technical and Further Education for every 100 of the population in 1976, as compared with four per 100 in Victoria. This year the total enrolment will exceed the total enrolment for Victoria, although South Australia has only a third of Victoria's population.

Australians are coming to accept that learning is a lifelong process, and that those who abandon it can rarely live full and satisfying lives as citizens or as human beings. Education is for life and is lifelong, and more Australians are celebrating that fact.